I0425641

PTSD
RECOVERY+

FROM SORROW TO GLORY
ATOZ
GUIDE ON OVERCOMING PTSD
(POST-TRAUMATIC STRESS DISORDER)
EASILY

Dr.Paul A. Williams

Legal & Disclaimer

Testimonials

Thank you for the excellent knowledge you have provided me with, from your book I came to realize that my daughter was struggling with PTSD disorder which she kept silent with but now she is on therapy and now recovering – **Y. K.**

As a military soldier who has served for over thirty years your book have helped me a lot, it is until I read your book is when I realized I was suffering from PTSD disorder and now am on treatment and doing well – **Col. J. S.**

Am able now to manage my flashbacks and the traumatic event memories I experienced when I got my self-involved in a plane crash in Australia when I was expecting my firstborn child which I lost the pregnancy due to the accident. Have been able to do away with the flashbacks since I read your book – **L. G.**

Hello from your book, I realized that also children undergo PTSD, from the events they experience or witnessed, this also depends on what we expose our children to while they develop. For example, if they watch their parents fighting each day, this might expose them to PTSD. Thank you very much for your book – **M. K.**

I thank you so much, am a professional psychologist but have learned a lot from your book, and now I will be able to handle my clients with great care and to deliver the appropriate treatment – **Dr. M. C.**

Am left with only an option of reading your book regularly because I remember my friends who are the victims of PTSD and I try to help them just from the knowledge from your book, I am grateful and will always look for your books – **P. S.**

Am struggling to recover from my PTSD symptoms which I have found, have been isolating myself from my friends. Through your book, I have gained coping skills and now can interact with my friends freely. I love this book – **V. J.**

Thanks a lot for your book. I am from Canada and have been helping my husband heal from PTSD symptoms like flashbacks. My husband has been having a problem sleeping due to nightmares from the traumatic event he experienced now he can sleep without any nightmare at all. Thanks a lot for your book – **M. S.**

Your book act as means of treatment to me. I have learned that PTSD can be still treated and that it's not a lifetime disease. I'm a military guy who has been in Iraq for a mission for several years andhas hope that one day I will heal properly. I salute you for an excellent job you are doing – **Wing Cdr. S. K.**

Table of Contents

Chapter 5

Chapter 6

Chapter 7

INTRODUCTION

Personal Stories

Story 1

Jane was only 13 when she came across the attackers. She was attacked by a group of men when she was from school. They screamed at her with each raping her in turns and almost stubbing her if the police could not reach the scene in time. Several months after the terrible experience Jane could not control herself, the memories of the attack could not get out of her mind when sleeping at night, and she could have fearful dreams of being raped and streaming from the attackers. Jane could not walk to school comfortably, and every time she walks towards the scene place she could start crying and find for another long route Jane could use, Jane felt she has reached to the end of life she could not control her emotions anymore. At home, Jane was lonely and felt very dirty to interact with the fellow, very anxious and tensed much, and she felt not to tell her friends because she thought she could face rejection. Jane could struggle with the memories for a very long time until that time. She decided to open up and share the story with the art teacher.

Story 2

James was experienced and active combat at his time in the military; some of the activities he witnessed has not gone out of his mind. One of the most horrible scenes was when his close friend was blown up by a land mine. Even when he is not at work these images disturbed him so much, the images and memories of the war events came across his mind almost every time disrupting his attention from work, at some times when he is at the filling stations and smells diesel this could trigger some of the memories. Most of the times, he could not remember what had just happened a few minutes ago because of the deep think of the minds when he was serving as a soldier, the memories were painful to remember back. Most of the times, he could avoid military friends not to trigger the memories. The girlfriend complained of her irritability, James could not have a relaxed night, and anytime he hears loud noises he could jump as if he is ready to combat and started to drink heavily as a coping skill.

Chapter 1

Post-traumatic Stress Disorder (PTSD)

Post-traumatic stress disorder (PTSD) is a mental illness that usually occurs when a person is a victim or has just witnessed a horrible, traumatic, tragic, or any scaring events. Those who suffer from the PTSD experiences persistent frightening thoughts and memories of the traumatic events and emotionally numb to close friends. It is an anxiety problem that people experience after a traumatic event such as combat, sexual abuse, crime, and natural disaster. The people living with PTSD will always try to not to associate with anything that reminds them about the trauma. Those who are suffering from PTSD may be feeling fine at some moments and after sometimes they are drawn to deep thoughts trying to relieve themselves from the traumatic events, which results to other disorders such as anxiety. PTSD occurs in the following steps:

- Experience or witnessing the horrible activities and the physical threat is involved and fear.

- Experiencing the trauma many times in life.

- Trying to avoid anything related to the trauma, inability to remember the trauma, this can involve stopping socializing with your friends, controlling once emotions.

- Having sleep problems, lack of concentration at all and looking for other alternatives like drinking a lot.

- When symptoms last for more than one month.

- Not able to function properly in every day's life.

Types of PTSD

There are five main types of PTSD that are very common and mostly experience. They include:

Normal Stress Response

It occurs to the adults who have experienced a single horrific trauma in their adulthood. Its comprised of bad memories of what happened to them, emotional numbing, they feel they are being cut off from a relationship or experience bodily distress. They can achieve recovery within a few weeks, and group debriefing may be appropriate to them. Most of them explore the survivor emotional responses to the traumatic events they experienced, and education offered on the survivor's response and positive ways for cooping provided.

Acute Stress Response

It comprises panic reactions, mental confusions dissociation, severe insomnia, guiltiness, and unable to manage self-care activities, relationships, and work. It is among the single survivors of the trauma but only when it is lastly exposing them to death, destructions. The primary treatment to this can be immediate support from the family and friends, removing the victim from the scene and use of medication as we will discuss later in the treatment.

Uncomplicated PTSD

Occurs when one re-experiences the traumatic activities that they, avoidance of the similar stimuli at any cost, the victims always try to avoid the incentives associated with the trauma, emotional numbing. Some of the treatment that can be applied are psychodynamics, cognitive-behavioral.

Comorbid PTSD

It is a combination of PTSD and other disorders, mostly experienced than the other disorders like uncomplicated PTSD. PTSD is usually associated with major psychiatric disorders like anxiety, substance abuse, and panic attacks. It is much appropriate to treat both the diseases together and not one after other for example PTSD and substance abuse can be treated together, the same treatment used in uncomplicated PTSD used for the patients with the additional psychiatric disorders.

Complex PTSD

Also known as the Disorder of Extreme Stress, among the individuals who have experienced or witnessed the traumatic events for a very long period, since their childhood like sexual abuse by the relatives or any other person. They also suffer borderline personality disorders, and they have problems when exhibiting their behaviors in cases such as aggression, impulsivity, eating disorders and sexuality, and alcohol and substance abuse. Difficulties are expressing their emotions. The treatments for such patients usually take a long time because of their slow progress, and they require the most critical and sensitive treatment methods and experts in the trauma treatments.

Myths and Facts about PTSD

There are some beliefs that people have about PTSD, but they are not true, some of the myths include:

- All the people that have experience or witness life-threatening activities will develop PTSD. Most people who usually experienced or see traumatic events do not suffer PTSD.

Those who have PTSD are less than 10% of those who have been exposed to traumatic events for more than a year, with 37% exposed to internal trauma.

- Only those who are week get PTSD. It has not clear why some people will get PTSD and others don't understand, women are at high risk of getting PTSD compared to men, this is because women are ready to seek for help making them prepared to be diagnosed with more disorders compared to men. Those exposed to interpersonal trauma like sexual abuse or domestic violence are more likely to get PTSD than those who survive from accidents or other natural disasters like earthquakes.

Symptoms and coping myths

- After some time, I should be able to work on my trauma. Traumas are always dominant, but they are within as a person can be doing well and functioning appropriately, but something triggers the memories and symptoms comes out. As people grow old, they also lose their minds exposing them to older memories, and in case some of the memories were traumatic events then they find themselves at a problem of being bothered by the memories from the decades.

- My trauma was of a long time ago, and I can't do anything about it now. At any stage, it's never too late to handle your trauma. Most people feel their childhood trauma like sexual abuse when they are adults, but still, they heal correctly — treated as a group with the same traumatic event than when handled individually and the game was less than a year ago. Finds when most of their identity about the trauma has settled and significant impact in their lives.

- Should be handling my trauma myself. Most people will struggle with their injury alone and seek for help later when now it's too much for them, and men will not reach out for help and struggle with the trauma alone because our culture makes as to believe that men are powerful and should not seek for help for such issues. Asking for help doesn't mean that one is very lazy to handle the situation alone but just seeking for support and sharing of experience from those who have experienced the same or experts to help as come up with the coping skills which may not be dangerous to our lives later.

PTSD Therapy Myths

- I am so anxious and want to process the trauma, and everything will be okay. The treatment is a process and requires patience for someone to heal, this is because for one to seek for help the memories are rooted in their thoughts, and it will sometimes need to get out the memories. The treatment agreed upon has protocols and steps:

1. Safety and coping

2. Review of the horrific memories

3. Integration

- If I can't remember the trauma, then I can't solve it. There other therapies that can be used that do not need one to recall the traumatic events that they experienced or they witnessed like the evidence-based therapy, and the treatment assumes that the trauma is stored in the body and the survivor is helped to connect what the body is feeling.

Chapter 2

Parts of the Brain that are Affected by the Trauma

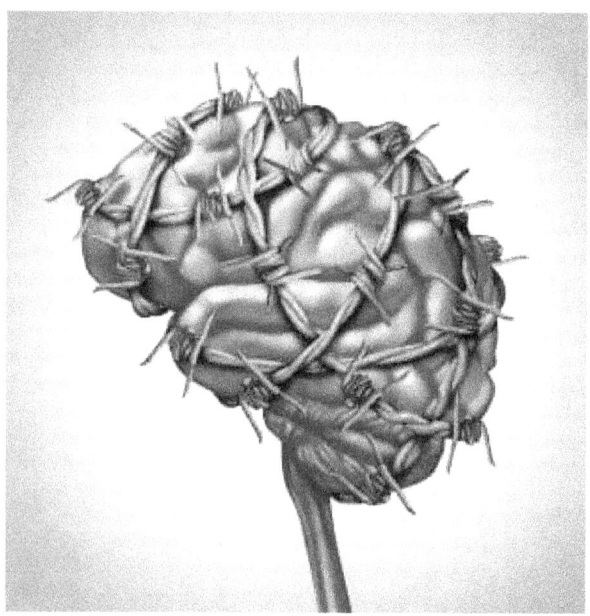

Averagely 50% of people will experience traumatic activities at some stage in their lives, but they do not suffer PTSD. The trauma we experience or witness change the functions of the brain at some point more so when someone close to as is struggling to live with their injury. The traumatized brain will coordinate things differently due to the traumatic events they have recorded, the mind is plastic, and it can be changed.

How trauma alters the brain functioning and the parts affected

1. **The prefrontal context**, this is the thinking center and is located near the behind the forehead it is responsible for the abilities to reason, problem-solving skills, personality, planning and it also makes us aware of ourselves and others. When this part of the brain is functional, we can think clearly and make the right decisions have self-awareness and our environment.

2. **The anterior cingulate**, it is located just next to the prefrontal cortex but inside the brain. It regulates our emotions and works jointly with the thinking center. When the part is functional, we can manage stressful thoughts that we are experiencing, and also used for regulating the emotions without being overcome by the feelings and emotions, and this helps us not to participate in the activities that will make us regret later in our lives.

3. **And the amygdala,** the thin structure found in our brains which act as a fear center, its primary function is to receive information from all our perception organs, and it detects any threat that might be present in our environment and produces fear.

The traumatized brain looks more different compared to the non-traumatized mind

1. The thinking center is under activated

2. The anterior cingulate is under enabled

3. Amygdala is over-activated

Causes of PTSD

Researchers have not concluded the exact cause of PTSD for those who suffer from it; people experience or witness traumatic events, but not all those who experience it suffer PTSD. It is likely a combination of factors that contribute to this, including genetics, personality, life experience, stress, and neurological that provide to other people who have PTSD. The focus to find the cause for PTSD has been its impact on the brain, and it focuses on how the traumatic events have affected the brain functions. Researchers suggest that being overwhelmed by the traumatic events makes the mind not to process any information and not feeling in the right conditions. The traumatic events take control of intruding consciousness, which causes much distress.

There are pre-traumatic psychological factors that may trigger the disorder like low self-esteem, which can worsen the situation. Low self-esteem, which may have been sexually abused, may is much exposed to the PTSD. Post-traumatic reactions from close friends and relatives towards the victims affect them very much, for example, a raped lady is seen as dirty and unclean by the close relatives this causes physical discomfort and flashbacks of the rape events and may influence the persistence of the symptoms. The study of the brain and the mind and its chemical have helped scientist with much information on how the components of the brain and memory contribute to the development of PTSD.

The brain study did focus on the significant two structures of the brain that is: the amygdala and the hippocampus. Amygdala is responsible for fear of how we detect fear in our environment, and it is much hyperactive in those who have PTSD. While the hippocampus is responsible for the formation of memories, there is some placed evidence that those who have PTSD have a loss of volume in the structure and this contributes to the deficits of mind and most of the symptoms of PTSD. Other studies conducted on the neurochemicals that are involved in the cause of PTSD. Hypothalamic pituitary adrenal which is a hormone which is believed to be interrupted within those who have PTSD. It is included in the stress reaction at reasonable rates and its disruption, and its disorder conceptualized as a false alarm.

Hypothalamic pituitary adrenal (HPA) when it is not functional, it re3suts to the damage of hippocampal in those who have PTSD. Medication to this dysfunction reverse to neurochemical dysfunction in those who have PTSD, and they act as agents that switch off the false alarm. It is possible to predict the development of PTSD on early psychological and neurological changes that occur in people exposed to traumatic events.

Risk factors for PTSD

There are numbers of factors that expose people to PTSD, and put people at a higher chance to get PTSD. They include

- Experience or witness a loss at early childhood; this can consist of buses and neglect from families and close relatives or the unknown people.
- Experienced long-lasting trauma, a trauma that does not end, and memories keep on coming to our consciousness.

- Witnessed or underwent severe trauma, like sexual abuse from a close relative or parents during childhood.

- When you view or read a history of mental illness awareness that others are suffering from in their lives.

- You are being in situations that put you at higher risk of harm like your environmental work situations, for example, those working in the military.

- Experience history of substance or drug abuse like alcohol, this happens when one wants to withdraw from the situation or uses drug abused as coping skills from PTSD.

- History of the mental illness among the family members, genetics where we acquire the genes from our parents. If a parent had PTSD, there is a likely hood that the genes passed to the children.

- When some families or close relatives and friends rely on each other for emotional support, but still they don't get the help from the people they trust.

PTSD Diagnostic and Statistical Manual (DSM)

PTSD wan recognized as a mental illness in 1980, then it was included in the DSM for mental disorders, there was much debate about the disease, but researchers concluded that it is a mental disorder. This was because most of the researchers believed that emotional disturbance after experiencing a traumatic event was regular, but to some people, it results in PTSD and others it did not occur to this PTSD.

PTSD in the DSM-5 Criteria

In DSM-IV and DSM-5, there have been many changes on PTSD, but currently, there are only eight criteria to conclude that someone has PTSD. The first criteria are as follows:

- When one directly experiences the traumatic events. When you interact with the traumatic event straight, for example, sexual abuse or get involved in an accident.

- Witnessing personally the traumatic events how it happened to others, observing how the horrific events happened to a relative, friend or somebody else.

- Getting to know that the traumatic event happened to a close friend, family member, or relatives.

- Re-experiencing traumatic events or too much exposure to traumatic events.

The second criteria for PTSD, which comprises of symptoms involving having repeated of the following:

- Perceptions of our environments

- Images of the traumatic events

- Scary dreams

- Too many illusions and hallucinations, perceiving things that do not exist.

- Flashbacks of the traumatic events that are dissociated.

- Severe psychological distress or anticipating of events to happen.

The third criteria that involve the avoidance of the same stimuli to the traumatic event, avoiding anything that reminds as of the traumatic events.

- Avoiding the thoughts, any feelings, or not talking about the traumatic events we experience.

- Avoiding the factors that might trigger the traumatic memories like avoiding the places, people, or not engaging in any activities that will remind as of the traumatic events we experienced.

The fourth criteria are all about the persistent negative thoughts about traumatic activities.

- One is unable to remember significant events in life, even the once that have been just completed.

- Persistent and overrated negative perceptions about ourselves, others, and our environment.

- Continuously scattered thoughts about the cause of the traumatic event.

- Continuously negative emotional moods.

- Loss of interest to participate in various activities

- Loss of attention from family and friends, feeling detached

- Continuously unable to show positive emotions.

The fifth criteria involve increment of the arousal rates and reactivity

- Displaying irritable behaviors and get angry more often, becomes more irritated very quickly and cannot handle the angry outburst.

- Engages in de3scructive activities as a coping skill.

- Hypervigilance, which increases anxiety.

- Sleep problems have sleep problems not able to sleep properly because of horrific dreams and flashback at night, which are very scary.

- Difficulties in concentrating, attention span is minimal

- Overrated startle response.

And the remaining three criteria

- When the duration of the symptoms is more than 1month, in case the signs are witnessed for more than one month then it can be concluded that the person is suffering from PTSD

- When the disturbances from the memories result in more distress and not able to perform correctly in our daily activities.

- When the disturbance is not as a result of other medical conditions or substance abuse.

Symptoms required to diagnose one who has the PTSD will depend on the criteria listed above.

Chapter 3

Signs and Symptoms of PTSD

PTSD is a mental illness that is mostly characterized by symptoms of avoidance and nervous system arousal after experiencing or witnessing the horrific events. Apart from the military soldiers who serve as combat with much exposer to the traumatic events, also those who suffer or see accidents and injuries, rape and sexual abuse have PTSD in their lives. For one to be diagnosed with PTSD, there are signs and symptoms that must be seen or displayed by the victims for more than one month, and the symptoms should have impacts on their daily functioning and required age limit for one to be diagnosed which is seven years and above. The symptoms include:

1. Traumatic event symptoms

One exposed to the threatening event by either experiencing it or witnessing the trauma. For example, one may hear of close friends or relatives who suffered from traumatic events

- ❖ Death
- ❖ Serious injuries
- ❖ Sexual abusei

❖ Intrusion symptoms

This is when one re-experiences the traumatic events most of the time. They include:

- Memories of the traumatic event that happened to them.

- Sleepless nights due to the traumatic events.

- Flashbacks, they imagine that the trauma is happening again.

- Psychological and physical avoidance of traumatic reminders such as the places where

the event took place, not talking about the event.

2. Avoidant symptoms

- Always avoid thoughts related to the trauma

- Avoiding friends, or situations that remind as of the shock

3. Unstable negative moods

There is a decline in thoughts patterns or attitudes. They include:

- Much difficulties in memory which are not part of the traumatic event.

- Negativity about one's self or the environment.

- Distorted sense of blame for the traumatic event for one's self or others.

- Not able to handle the server emotions that are as a result of the traumatic event. Like

  sadness and shame.

- Loss of interest in the pre-traumatic activities

- Isolates from friends

Increased arousal symptoms

These symptoms describe the state of the brain. They include:

- Cannot concentrate

- Irritable and outburst anger

- Sleeping problems

- Hypervigilance

- Being easily startled.

4. 6,7and 8 criteria, these show the severity of the symptoms named, the symptoms must last for at least one month. The symptoms must affect one's ability to function in daily life and not associated with substance use or any other medical conditions.

Dissociation

They are separated from symptoms. They include:

- Depersonalization

- Hallucination.

Signs of PTSD

Though DSM-5 is evident on the symptoms of the PTSD, still there is an additional sign that can suggest PTSD. They include the following:

- Destructive behaviors like drug abuse

- Feeling emotionally numb

- Unable to maintain a close relationship

- Shame

- Hallucinations.

Those who have PTSD are also at risk of suffering from:

- Panic attack
- Agoraphobia
- Obsessive-compulsive disorder
- Phobia and anxiety
- Major depressive disorders
- Somatization disorders
- Suicide

Chapter 4

Treatments for PTSD

There are only two main primary treatment methods used for treating those who have PTSD. They include:

1) Psychotherapy for PTSD

2) Medication for PTSD

Psychotherapy for PTSD

The most appropriate treatment for those who have PTSD is psychotherapy and done through individual therapy, individual therapy, or both. Most of the victims who have PTSD exposed to traumatic events, which is called exposure therapies and considered the most effective.

The exposure done in various ways, such as trauma-focused cognitive behavioral therapy, another type of treatment used is reprocessing therapy. They are all evidence-based therapie3s that have worked according to the researchers.

Though the therapies are the most effective treatments for the PTSD, trauma symptoms are particular, and not all the medicines will be appropriate. The therapy treatments still overlap in various ways, which include:

❖ Most of the therapy helps trauma victims with proper coping skills, which are related to the symptoms. They include emotional intelligence, thoughts restructuring, relaxation, and psychoeducation on the signs and symptoms of the type of trauma they experienced or witnessed.

❖ For proper treatment, one needs to revisit the trauma they experienced, and this is through retelling the story reprocess the memories which will allow the body to relive.

❖ The therapies are carried out in groups or as individuals or even both.

❖ For the exploration of one's trauma, you need to have some stability. Avoid free addiction, suicidal ideation, which will have a significant impact on security while dealing with the injury. It is not a must for life to be perfect, but an individual need to see some improvement in the ways they deal with their trauma.

Trauma Therapy

There are phases that one needs to complete in the treatment of trauma as recommended by the experts.

Phase 1: To achieve the patient's safety, minimizing symptoms and enhancing competence

This is the skill-building phase, and the clinician is free to use evidence-based therapies to improve on the emotions, distress, tolerance, thoughts, and actions restructuring. The step is beneficial as it can help someone to move from the trauma to the next stage.

Phase 2: revisit the reappraisal of the trauma flashbacks

Any success in this phase promotes the ability to patient discomfort from the flashbacks of the injury, and it is appropriate for those who suffered a single traumatic event, while those who suffered complex trauma may undergo this for several months before they get ready to process their trauma.

Phase 3: Consolidating gains

The role of the therapist at this stage is to help the client to apply and adopt new coping skills and have self-awareness and their trauma experience. This phase act as booster session for the coping skills, promoting professionalism, support, and care plan for the victims.

Let's explore Trauma Therapies

Exposure Therapy

Happens is when an individual exposed to the traumatic event they experienced or witnessed over and over for years until the horrific event is no longer activating in their minds. A military officer can use this therapy as they can talk about their experiences until it stops activating. Trauma-Focused Cognitive Behavioral Therapy, used in children and adolescence, it is a narrative that is used to expose the victims to the traumatic events they experienced witnessed. Cognitive processing therapy can also include narrative trauma strategies.

- The exposure did once; this will help build a tolerance.
- The trauma narratives did through the word of mouth or use of art forms such as images.
- The therapies can only apply to those who have experienced single traumatic events, or they might have experienced several events but do not have any other mental illness.

The cognitive processing therapy is suitable for those who have served at the military.

Eye Movement Desensitization and Reprocessing (EMDR)

This therapy helps the individual to reprocess their memories and the events experienced, the individual able to access the relevant memory and use dual awareness, image, thoughts, emotions, and body perception to resolve the traumatic experiences that were not addressed. EMDR allows those who have PTSD to put everything into control and organized them so that the non-traumatic memories have not interfered with at any point.

- This form of therapy recommended to those with developmental or complex disorder trauma.

- EMDR has phases of treatments that it uses, with the focus on building skills and resourcing for the process phase.

EMDR is much useful for private and groups, this because it helps in the cognitive reprocessing.

Somatic Therapies

Uses the body to process the trauma, though it is considered none evidence based because no much research has been done to it to support it. Most of the cases it has been used in individuals but still can be applied to groups. The use of body symptoms to help those who are suffering from PTSD, group therapy, is much appropriate for the individuals who experienced trauma in their lives or witnessed any horrific events. This will help to prevent isolation due to the symptoms they are possessing.

Choosing the most appropriate treatment for you.

Like any therapy finding the appropriate and trusted therapist is essential for the healing process. Your therapist should be open to you and clear on their treatment methods and plans, good therapy will enable you to work with them to see some progress in your symptoms as you heal. Always ask questions when you have any about your treatment methods, and you are free to seek for referrals in case you feel uncomfortable with the progress of your treatment.

Psychotherapy will take a long time before any impact seen, one needs to be patient as the therapy will start to work maybe after 2-3 months, and more benefits from the treatment seen as time go by even after the sessions with the therapist.

Some psychotherapy will involve temporary discomfort, maybe when talking or thinking about the trauma. But you need to be able to handle the comforts and get help from your therapy on how to feel the discomfort.

Medication for PTSD

Medication is used together with the psychotherapy for the treatment of PTSD, the medicines are only to treat the symptoms that are associated with the disorder like the anxiety and depression, but they cannot relieve one from the traumatic flashbacks. While one decides to receive medication from their specialist, they also need to seek referrals from to the psychotherapist, and this will enable complete healing from the traumatic events.

Antidepressants

The most medication prescribed for the people living with PTSD are the selective serotonin reuptake inhibitor antidepressants, they comprise drugs such as fluoxetine, sertraline, and paroxetine. The medicine helps in the treatment of anxiety, depression, and panic that are related to PTSD in many people. They also help to reduce aggression, impulsivity, and suicidal ideation that people who have PTSD.

The medications start to work from the 6-8 week and not immediately, and much patience may be needed while one starts to use the medicines. Most of the people with PTSD don't respond to the medication the first time they use them and need the second antidepressant once the first attempt fails to work. It may not be easy for the relapse to occur when the medication prescribed for not less than one year.

The antidepressants are useful for those suffer depression at the same, but the drug is still active even in the absence of the depression, they are helping those having abuse of alcohol and other substance abuse in their history.

Other Medications

There are other alternatives apart from antidepressants that can be used to reduce the symptoms that are related to PTSD with the common one being atypical antipsychotics, and they include medication such as risperidone, olanzapine, and quetiapine. The antipsychotic is very useful to the people living with PTSD who also suffer from agitation, dissociation, hypervigilance, paranoia. Mood stabilizers used in the treatment of PTSD they include: lamotrigine, Gabitril, and Depakote. The medication that helps to reduce the physical symptoms that are related PTSD include the following: clonidine, propranolol, and Tenex.

Benzodiazepines used as sleeping tablets, minor tranquilizer, or antianxiety medication are also prescribed to decrease some PTSD symptoms, this is because they provide relief of anxiety, but still antidepressants are used much compared to them. The drug is to be prescribed by the psychiatrist.

Chapter 5

The best diet for PTSD patients

These are the best five foods that will help relieve PTSD.

1. Blueberries

Research has shown that blueberries reduce or lower the symptoms of PTSD in rats. Blueberries help in controlling moods and increasing the levels of serotonin in the brain, which helps in relieving PTSD.

2. Cheese and Milk

These are rich in an amino acid known as tyrosine, which can trigger the production of dopamine, epinephrine, and norepinephrine. These help to increase the levels of energy and alertness in the body. Which has whey protein which acts stress antidote?

3. Chamomile Tea

Chamomile has properties that help in fighting stress, and it has a calming effect on those who frequently get irritated, depressed agitation, and mood swings.

4. Walnuts

Walnuts produce omega-three fatty acids. People who lack omega in their body are very pessimism, depressive symptoms, and impulsive actions. They are much different from the greasy foods which will worsen the situation, making one to feel sluggish and fatigue.

5. Green Vegetables

Kales and spinach are rich in folic acid, which defends as from the causes of depression mostly in men. Other foods which can help in this are nuts, sprout, and oranges.

The best exercise for PTSD patients

There has been evidence showing activity is suitable for those who have PTSD, this is because it helps in the treatment of the disorder, some good exercise can help to regulate moods, minimize anxiety and relive more stress. Mind-body and low- intensity both have positive impacts on depression and its symptoms and depression.

Designing an exercise program for PTSD patients

Presences of other mental disorder in those who have PTSD is a significant barrier to the effective exercise for PTSD. These include depression, substance abuse, physical injuries suffered as the result of traumatic events will have much effect on the exercise plan, right exercise professionals will help their clients to over the barriers and to motivate them.

When planning for the best exercise for the clients it is good to deal with the clients individually because of their personal needs, and always there should be low-intensity and the body awareness activities like Pilates, Yoga, Nia, and Therapeutic dance. They help to reduce the symptoms of anxiety and depression on the PTSD suffers. Diaphragmatic breathing regularly and muscles relaxations will help in the natural calmness effect.

Pleasant environment for the exercise matters a lot, and it should be free from noise or any other trigger to the traumatic event to allow the patient focus on activity, patients whom who display fatigue symptoms because of the antidepressants they use should not participate much in exercise as this will worsen their situation.

Patients with avoidance or withdrawal symptoms need special treatment when planning for their exercise plan, and they need to have their exercise in private

with face to face instructor as this helps them build confidence and starts to interact with the small groups as they continue healing.

Ten key factors to consider a professional when designing an exercise program for PTSD clients

1. Be Repetitive, and this will help the client to master the exercise.

2. Be predictability, and this will help minimize the anxiety that triggers PTSD memories.

3. Do not have a competitive environment, and the competitive environment can activate the sympathetic nervous system, which results in more stress. The main goal of exercise in PTSD is to reduce pressure.

4. Be reflective, helps the clients to be aware of their body's response to stress hence becoming capable of handling their stress.

5. Have patience, wait for the impacts of the exercise which will not start immediately.

6. Be realistic, be open and honest while developing the exercise plan to your clients.

7. Be flexible, help the client to handle situations that might arise; this will help them heal properly.

8. Don't judge, as a professional expert in PTSD exercise planning understands your client to avoid judging, which can demoralize them.

9. Be prepared, be ready to listen and to care for your clients. Talk your clients

10. Have much knowledge, be updated in the changes of medication, and have them at your fingertips.

Chapter 6

Assessment for PTSD

Interviews and self-report are the most tools used in the evaluation of PTSD

Interviews

Clinical-Administered PTSD Scale

This is a 30 item structured interview, and it is used to make a diagnosis, assess PTSD in the previous weeks. It lasts for about 40-60 minutes. The meeting is used by clinicians and clinical researcher with in-depth knowledge in PTSD.

PTSD Symptoms Scale Interview

It is a 17 item structured interview used for diagnosis, the respondents with the traumatic events identify one traumatic event that distresses them then the system assessed in the last two weeks. It lasts for about 20 minutes, with only one question with no follow-up question.

Structured Clinical Interview; PTSD Module

The instrument is administered by a trained mental professional, where all the symptoms are recorded as present, subthreshold, and absent, and it depends on the interviewee's personal experience, and it last for several hours.

Structured Interview for PTSD

Used to assess PTSD symptoms that correspond to DSM- IV and the observation of the survival and behavioral guilt. The symptoms are rated as for the past r4 weeks, and the instrument also measures the frequency and intensity of the symptoms. It is administered for about 20-30 minutes.

Self-report instruments that can be used include

Davidson Trauma Scale

The scale has 17 items that are used to assess the 17 DSM symptoms, and it measures both the frequency and severity of the symptoms. Others include:

- Impact of the Event Scale

- Mississippi Scale for Combat-related PTSD.

- Modified PTSD Symptoms Scale

- PTSD Checklist for DMS-5

- PTSD Symptoms Scale Self-Report Version

- Short PTSD Rating Interview

PTSD Screening Quiz

These are an online quiz that one can take to help them assess themselves; they have instant answers after taking the exam, one can go and see a professional for further assistant. The questionnaire only takes about 1-2 minutes to complete. For example:

Instructions: *Below are some of the stressful problems that people undergo, due to traumatic events they experience, please go through each question and indicate appropriately the response that has been bothering you for the last one month.*

I am a……. years old   Female   Male   Other

1. **Have been experiencing repeated, thoughts, images, and disturbing memories in the past?**

   Never

   Rarely

   Sometimes

   Often

   Very Often

2. **Feeling so irritated when reminded of the past stressful memories?**

   Never

    Rarely

   Sometimes

   Often

   Very Often

3. **Always avoiding the triggers that remind me of the stressful events in the past?**

   Never

   Rarely

   Sometimes

   Often

   Very Often

4. Feeling isolated from others?

Never

Rarely

Sometimes

 Often

 Very Often

5. Unable to control my angry outburst?

Never

Rarely

Sometimes

Often

Very Often

6. Unable to concentrate?

Never

Rarely

 Sometimes

 Often

Very Often

Scoring Key

14 and above   PTSD can be available

10-13   PTSD possible

0-9   No disorder

Chapter 7

PTSD in Children

PTSD can also occur in children, and traumatic events can happen to anybody regardless of their age and in response to the traumatic event.

Causes of PTSD in children

- Watching their parents killed
- Witnessing a sexual assault
- Involved in sexual abuse
- Experiencing school shooting
- Seeing any form of violence next to their home.

PTSD in Rape and Abuse Victims

Rape and abuse are much common and are against human beings. They violate the survivor's self-esteem and interfere with the safety of the victims leading to the development of PTSD.

According to the National Center for PTSD, 2015

- Almost 94% will experience PTSD symptoms after two weeks of the assault
- A third of the victims of rape will still show PTSD symptoms after nine months.
- 3.8million women will develop PTSD at the stage in their lives.
- 11% of rape victims will develop chronic PTSD

PTSD in Rape Victims and their reactions

- Disorganization

- Shock and disbelief

- Physical health problems

- Lifestyle change.

PTSD in Military Veterans

The effect of PTSD on the veterans is similar to the general population, but with slightly different for instance, 95% of the veterans in Iraq have watched the dead bodies and 93% have been shoot.

The number of veterans who suffer from PTSD will depend on the area they are employed to serve. In operation in Iraq, the percentage of veterans affected by PTSD was between 11-20%

The symptoms of the PTSD on the veterans are similar to the rest of the population like

- Re-experiencing the traumatic event

- Avoidance of anything that triggers the memories.

- Anger outburst

- Change in thoughts, feelings related to the trauma that is always negative.

Some of the believes that veterans have that prevent them from seeking help includes:

- Will be seen weak

They should have different treatment with the general population.

- Losing confidence in them

- Their privacy matters

- They trust family and friends for their help

- Don't believe in the treatment

- They have much concern about the side effect of the procedure that might interfere with their work

- Concern over the cost and the location of the treatment

How long does PTSD last

There has been a debate about along should the disorder last, with the answer varying in person to person. The cause of the trauma matters and how the individuals respond to the events.

Factors that will influence the duration of PTSD

- Chronic trauma vs. one traumatic event.

- Was the trauma experienced knowingly or it was accidentally.

- Was the trauma-induced or it was as a result of the natural disaster.

- Was the trauma a sexual or not sexual.

Life-related factors that will influence the duration of PTSD

- History of other horrific events

- Having other mental disorders

- Social support you receive

- The therapy we receive

According to DSM-5

- Half of the adults who have PTSD recovered fully within three months

- But in different PTSD last for more than three months but less than one year.

- For some, it can last for more than 12 months, and in others, it can last for more than 50 years.

THANK YOU

Thank you for reading **PTSD Recovery+**. I as an author, really appreciate that you read the book and you showed your trust in me**. It really means a lot to me**. I wish you the best of luck in your life ahead and I really hope that you recover from PTSD. I value the connection we have established through this book and I will make sure that I keep bringing value on the table.

I would appreciate your honest review and rating on Amazon

Review here: https://www.amazon.com/dp/B07VXY7F2C

If you have any questions or you want me to help you in your life or think that I can do something for you, you can reach out to me via email,

e-mail: drpaulawilliamsbook@gmail.com